AF255816

Schizophrenia and Suicide

Schizophrenia and Suicide

FINDING HOPE,
MEANING, AND DIRECTION

Marcia A. Murphy

Foreword by Del D. Miller

RESOURCE *Publications* · Eugene, Oregon

SCHIZOPHRENIA AND SUICIDE
Finding Hope, Meaning, and Direction

Resource Publications
An Imprint of Wipf and Stock Publishers
199 W. 8th Ave., Suite 3
Eugene, OR 97401

www.wipfandstock.com

PAPERBACK ISBN: 978-1-6667-6918-0
HARDCOVER ISBN: 978-1-6667-6919-7
EBOOK ISBN: 978-1-6667-6920-3

Contents

To all the healthcare professionals in Emergency Departments,
what is known by many as the ER

I am the light of the world;
he who follows me will not walk in darkness,
but will have the light of life.

—John 8:12b RSV

Foreword

MARCIA MURPHY, THE AUTHOR of this handbook, is a person who had the onset of serious mental illness, specifically schizophrenia and depression, in her teen years. She, like others with serious mental illnesses, struggled immensely with her illness. She lost meaning and purpose in her life and at age thirty-nine attempted to end her life by suicide. She depicts her life experiences that brought her to a point of severe desolation and feeling that life was no longer worth living. She eloquently describes her feelings that led to her taking an overdose of her medications to end her torment, and the experiences of being in the emergency room and then regaining consciousness in the intensive care unit. Fortunately, her life and story do not end there. Marcia is a talented writer who communicates her struggles and how she has overcome them in a way that conveys a clearer understanding of the struggles and needs of those experiencing mental illness and provides them hope and the knowledge that they are not alone on this journey.

How does a person who felt her life no longer had meaning or purpose, was hopeless, and attempted to end her life, come to write about suicide and how to overcome such inclinations? Over the years she has dedicated time and energy to seeking to understand her mental illness, what it meant for her life, and found what individuals with mental illness, their families, communities, and providers can do to improve their lives. She spent hours in libraries researching and reading about mental illness and writing about what she has learned over many years. Her work has opened doors of spirituality in the psychiatric community, helped religious groups to be better at accepting and incorporating those with mental illness, and has provided hope for others experiencing mental illness.

Suicide in serious mental illnesses like schizophrenia has and continues to be an enormous public health crisis. The prevalence of suicide in persons with schizophrenia is approximately five times that in the general population. There are assorted reasons that lead individuals with schizophrenia to want to end their lives. Schizophrenia often precludes individuals from having gainful employment and having normal social functioning and they are stigmatized. These lead to a lack of meaning in life, lack of satisfaction and self-worth, and social isolation. Even with advances in the treatment of schizophrenia, it continues to produce considerable suffering and far too often leads to suicide.

Marcia was able to move forward with her life in the face of continuing persistent symptoms of her illnesses. She has found that her religious beliefs, reading the Bible, prayer, attending worship services, writing, working to improve the lives of people with disabilities, and connecting with people, gives her life meaning, purpose, and hope, making it worth living. Not all of these may be helpful to every person with schizophrenia. Each person with schizophrenia has their own experiences but her story lets them know that there are others going through similar exercises. Her writing gives individuals with mental illness, families, mental health providers, and religious communities direction, inspiration, and hope.

Del Miller, Kathrine Griffin Professor of Psychiatry, University of Iowa Carver College of Medicine

Preface

One day, I was waiting at a bus stop at approximately 6:30 am. Clouds covered the sunrise which made visibility less. A streetlight lit up the road and I stood with my crutches at the bus stop across from my apartment building. I wore a heavy coat to compensate for the early fall lower 40-degree weather with a shoulder bag and heavy backpack on my back which held folders, pencils, and laptop.

There are two cats that live in the house to my left, up a ways across from the cement driveway, a white pick-up truck parked on the side of the green lawn. Just then, to my delight, one of the cats walked up to the property dividing fence, the one with a chest and shoulders of Siamese decent and the rest of its body and tail showing tabby breed. It seemed very mellow and sauntered over to the pole at the fence's endpoint and rubbed its side against it and then stood still and looked at me, I assume, thinking. I was thinking too: should I speak to the little animal or remain silent? Since I wasn't feeling very conversant, I just stood still and watched. Within a few seconds he/she slowly walked over and came close. It stretched out its head and rubbed its cheek against one of my crutch's poles, then its body; then it moved over and leaned against my left leg and rubbed with what I considered to be considerable affection. I was moved, emotionally, and said as I looked downward: "Nice kitty. Hi, kitty, kitty."

The cat went back and forth for a few seconds, rubbing against my leg; however, when I moved my crutches so that I could reach down and pet it with my hand, this frightened the cat some-what and it quickly stepped back a foot or so, but stopped there. I straightened up and was still. Then the cat moved forward and dropped to the ground; it laid down on its back exposing its tum-my, and curled, squirming its body around back and forth with its paws slightly bent, rubbing its back against the cement. I thought this was obviously an act of vulnerability and trust— exposing its underside to a human. I was flattered and became endeared to the cat. Then the bus pulled up and I got on.

When it comes to the subject of suicide it seems that the so-lution to the problem of self-destruction would be to find what personally makes our life worthwhile and to act on that. So then, what makes life worthwhile? Every day, every morning, I need to ask myself this question. Why get out of bed. Why take a bath or shower. Why get dressed and go out, ride the bus to . . . some-where. Somewhere to work or play, to socialize or to read. Explore ideas, places, people, and things. I am curious. Is curiosity a posi-tive trait? Depends on what we are curious about. It is bad to be curious about the wrong things. It's possible to go in the wrong direction. So, what gives us the right direction, our guidelines. If we have a Bible handy—I have one on a small table next to my livingroom chair—what does it say to do: daily, weekly, and for an extended period of time?

Social acceptance contributes to making life seem worth-while. How does the mentally ill person find friends? If we cannot love one another within church walls there will be injury of souls that God intended to receive his mercy and grace. If we cannot find God's love within the church then we will have to look else-where; for God will provide. Look in libraries or coffee shops, or riding on a city bus. Fellowship and love, somewhere, someplace. I sometimes find love in unexpected places that help to make me feel that life is worthwhile. For example, occasionally, from little furry friends.

Such brief encounters as with the neighborhood cat can make life seem worthwhile, at least for the moment or, potentially, longer, depending on the circumstance. In my book, *Schizophrenia*

& Suicide: Finding Hope, Meaning, and Direction, I share how as a person with schizophrenia, the thought of suicide, for me, and also for others with this disease, can be a constant threat to our well-being. In this book I explore the topic of survival for people who have a mental illness, for whom self-destruction through suicide is all too common in the age of medicines, psychotherapies, and peer counseling. In addition, what role do faith communities play in counteracting this affliction, and what are the responsibilities of the mentally ill, themselves, in choosing life over death by finding real meaning for their lives.

Acknowledgments

I WOULD LIKE TO thank the Saint Andrew Presbyterian Church Prayer Ministry group who have supported this work to its completion. Special recognition goes to my friend, Joan Van Hulzen, who has held me up with prayer for many years.

Thank you to all of you; I never would have made it this far without your prayerful support.

I

SUICIDE IN SCHIZOPHRENIA

PREVALENCE | REASONS

What is schizophrenia? Schizophrenia does not involve split or multiple personalities, as the general public believes. This is a misconception fueled by the mass media and Hollywood movies. Schizophrenia is an umbrella word for many kinds of symptoms, some of which are the following: thought disorder, hallucinations (auditory or visual), delusions, apathy, and withdrawal. A person may have some or all of these; individual cases vary enormously.[1]

People who have schizophrenia are nearly five times more likely to commit suicide than the general population.[2] Suicide is the 12th leading cause of death in the general population in the US; there were 45,979 deaths by suicide in US in 2020.[3]

- The suicide rate in the general population in 2020 was 13.48 per 100,000 individuals.

- In 2020, men died by suicide 3.88x more than women.

- On average, there are 130 suicides per day.

- White males accounted for 69.68% of suicide deaths in 2020.

- In 2020, firearms accounted for 52.83% of all suicide deaths.

Middle-aged adults (aged 35–64 years) account for 47.2% of all suicides in the United States, and suicide is the ninth leading cause of death for this age group.[4] People with schizophrenia are more likely to kill themselves when their illness is active, untreated, complicated, etc.[5] Illness-related risk factors are important

1. Murphy, *Collected Writings*, 44.

2. Palmer et al. "Lifetime Risk of Suicide," 247.

3. Shapiro, "Suicide Rates Spike in Spring," lines 4–5.

4. CDC, "Disparities in Suicide," para 5.

5. Hor and Taylor, "Suicide and schizophrenia," para 1.

predictors, with number of prior suicide attempts, depressive symptoms, active hallucinations, and delusions. The only consistent protective factor for suicide [among people with schizophrenia] according to the psychiatric field, was delivery of and adherence to effective treatment.[6] A family history of suicide, and comorbid substance misuse were also positively associated with later suicide. Generally speaking, in 2021, adults with [physical] disabilities were three times more likely to report suicidal ideation in the past month compared to persons without disabilities (30.6% versus 8.3% in the general U.S. population). Prior research has also reported on increased mental distress among this group [physical disability] which is a risk factor for suicide.[7] Reports show that 50 percent of chronic pain patients consider suicide to escape the unrelenting agony of their pain. A study published in *Psychosomatic Medicine* in 2006 found that relative to the general population, risk of death by suicide appears to be at least doubled in chronic pain patients.[8] As far as time periods during the year: contrary to popular belief, suicide rates go up for all categories of sufferers in the spring season, not winter.[9]

Why do these statistics show such a morbid and fatalistic response to sadness and despair? I will now discuss some of the reasons. For a portion of my life I was an unlikely candidate to write about the subject of suicide and how to overcome suicidal tendencies for my sympathies were disproportionately in the opposite camp. Why not kill yourself? Afterall, my first cousin on my father's side, Gayle, who had schizophrenia, committed suicide at the age of thirty-one. Perhaps now at this point in my life I will try to tackle the problem from the point of view as to why a person would want to kill oneself and what factors could possibly prevent it.

Generally speaking, the way humans treat one another has a huge impact on the emotional lives of all involved and can

6. Hor and Taylor, "Suicide and schizophrenia," para 1.

7. CDC, "Suicide Ideation and Disabilities," lines 2–5.

8. Paturel, "Treatment for Chronic Pain," para 5.

9. Shapiro, "Suicide Rates Spike in Spring," lines 4–5.

influence suicidal feelings and thoughts. How does society treat people who have schizophrenia and how does this affect the person who suffers from this mental condition? There are a lot of negative attitudes toward people with a schizophrenia diagnosis within the general population and also within the psychiatric community, itself, and this has a powerful influence on how patients feel about themselves.

Treating people as though they are not worthy of respect does, in fact, kill them. Treating people as though they are sub-human destroys a sense of worth to the point where they no longer wish to exist. Little by little such abusive treatment becomes internalized which can lead to negative behavior of recipients of this abuse of cigarette smoking, alcohol and/or illicit drugs, overeating, or deadly one-time successful lethal actions such as over-dose, hanging, or jumping from heights. Psychiatrists can prescribe all the antidepressant medications they want, but until the hidden and deeper psychological, societal, and spiritual issues are addressed biochemical remedies will, largely, fail. Sure, there may be a short-lived mood elevation; but in the long run medication treatments for depression will be unsuccessful because they don't get to source of the problem. I know, because I've been there; I tried antidepressants. As someone who has experienced schizophrenia and clinical depression, and with that, social rejection and ostracization, I have felt the numbing, apathetic hopelessness that leads to suicidal ideation (ideation: thoughts about taking one's own life). More than once in my life I attempted suicide. It was only by the grace of God that I was saved from an early death, a rescue partially attributed to specialized personnel in a hospital emergency department, God's instruments.

So, let us look now at possible reasons why a person may want to end their life. Many people who no longer wish to live have lost their sense of meaning and purpose. For some, it is an absence of a special relationship they once had. Or maybe it is a lack of employment or a project they would enjoy working on. Sometimes a person lacks a pet to take care of, a cat or dog. Or perhaps there are no hobbies like gardening to tend to, with its flowers, plants, and butterflies.

What happens when things in our daily lives no longer satisfy? When joy is lost in our endeavors? Entertainment is lifeless. Intellectual pursuits, boring and dry. We can no longer set goals or figure out how to achieve them. Everything seems futile. Why not stop getting up in the morning, why take a bath or shower? Why head out the door thinking we'll head to some interesting destination when there is none?

It has been my experience that when I believed in a higher power that was a step in the right direction; however, what did I conceive of as a god? Was it someone or a thing that loves me? Or was it fierce and cruel. Looking around the world with all its catastrophes we might imagine an unjust creator who brought the world into existence and then just stepped back and let it go wild. How, then, can we claim a loving god?

Most people who give up on life and end it just don't want to suffer anymore. They see no point in suffering. For many, they've reached the end of their rope and can't hang on anymore. Without turning to God as the answer, many tragedies take place. How do people function without a relationship with God? And how might this be related to the kind of mindset and lifestyle that leads a person toward self-destruction through suicide? In addition, how does the diagnosis of schizophrenia make everything worse?

First of all, when a person, any person, mentally ill or not, tries to live without God, what takes the place of God, that is, what becomes an idol? What would be an idol? Our main focus in life could be an idol: our spouse or romantic interest, a career, alcohol and drugs, overeating, pleasure and hedonism, money, power-seeking, or status. There are many kinds of idols, many varieties. All of these possibilities will form some type of mindset and pattern leading to habitual living patterns. If we fail, then, to find fulfillment or the idol eventually lets us down, the result could be catastrophic. Our emotional life can be devastated. We may no longer wish to live and start thinking of ways to end it all.

What we worship or idolize has its beginning in infancy. We all know that the family unit is where children learn their values which can either indicate a respect for God or not. In addition, do parents make a conscious effort to teach their children honesty, love, and respect for other human beings by word and deed? And within religious communities, do members do the same? What happens in the school systems, the everyday workplace, and civic organizations?

Sometimes a person may also contemplate suicide when their social life was at one time pleasant, but then falls apart. This may happen after falling into a relationship that was pleasant at first but then turns sour. Or sometimes, not knowing right from wrong socially, not knowing how to act in public. People may also have attitude problems such as a self-centered narcissism or an inflated ego. Such things are destructive in our human relationships.

Not only how we are treated by others, but a person's fundamental attitude toward other people is a factor in mental illness and suicide: is our attitude toward others malevolent or benevolent? Hostile, jealous, competitive, aggressive? Or inversely: loving, kind, thoughtful, empathetic, understanding? How do all these personality traits and mindsets influence whether we find life meaningful or the reverse—empty? Does one kind of outlook increase suicidal thoughts rather than the other?

And how do we perceive ourselves? Do we look upon ourselves with self-compassion and self-forgiveness? Do we have patience with ourselves when we fail or have other problems? Or do we harshly condemn ourselves. Has someone in our past taught us stern self-condemnation and harsh self-judgement? The way we feel about ourselves has a huge impact on whether we feel suicidal or not. Can we forgive what we see as our own failings and shortcomings and have patience with ourselves? In order to have patience with ourselves we need others around us to also be patient with us. One such supportive person was a psychiatrist I had who was a major influence in my adult life over a span of twenty-five years. Here is the correspondence from him in 1986 which reveals a caring, thoughtful person. I had written to him earlier to reestablish care after a brief separation of a few years:

Dear Marcia:

I received your letter of January 20, 1986. There is a great deal in it that we might talk about when I see you again. Let me just say that coping with an illness like schizophrenia is a very difficult task, and I respect you for what you have achieved in this regard. I agree that it is important for you to feel you have control over your life and that decisions you make are your own. You want to conserve your energies for making the best of a difficult situation and not expend them in fruitless struggles with family or others. For your own sake, you will want to function the best that you can within your limitations. Assessing these is never easy, but I think you have done pretty well at it.

The truth of the matter is, I think you have gotten along pretty well in recent years. Dr. Nelson and I agreed that this was how it appeared to us around the time of his retirement. At any rate, perhaps this is one of the things you will write about—the difficult task of coping with schizophrenia. I believe a book could be written about the subject.

Sincerely,
Russell Noyes, MD, Professor of Psychiatry
January 30, 1986

II

SUICIDE IN SCHIZOPHRENIA

EXPERIENCE | RESPONSE

It seemed a long walk to the convenience store. It was after 10 p.m. I went down the street oblivious to motorists and the extreme cold. At the store I took a bottle from the cooler and brought it to the cashier.

"A little wine for a fine evening?" he asked. I agreed and as I left, he added, "Enjoy!"

Walking back to my apartment it seemed to take even longer.

The antique goblet was lovely—probably seventy-five years old or more. It was so fragile. As I drank the wine I took a few Stelazines and then some Tofranil. I drank more wine and took more pills. At one point I put Robert's belongings outside my apartment door. I tore his nieces' drawings off the refrigerator and let them float to the floor.

Over the years I had not found answers to problems that had plagued me and I had no hope for the future. I only saw the dull repetition of crippling psychiatric symptoms and inhumane treatment by society—the never-ending humiliation of schizophrenia. My attempts to find meaningful relationships had not been successful, leaving me feeling empty and abandoned.

Maybe it was the fear of dying, I don't know, but at one point I scrambled for the phone book and found Dr. [Noyes's] number. I realized I'd be waking him. His wife answered in a subdued tone.

"Hello?"

"May I please speak with Dr. [Noyes]?"

"Yes . . . just a moment."

He came to the phone. It was about 12:30 a.m.

"Dr. [Noyes], this is Marcia Murphy . . . . "

From somewhere deep inside I felt a rising panic. I quickly explained what I had done and asked him what I should do. Not only did I realize I had no car but my sense of direction had begun to fade.

"What is your address? I'm going to call an ambulance," Dr. [Noyes] said in a steady voice.

I told him where I lived and soon an ambulance arrived and took me to the University Hospital Emergency Room. In the bright lights people seemed far away. A man in jeans, a physician, stood with his back to me. He was doing something with his hands and asked, "Why did you do it?"

"It's private."

That was it. Everything went black. I was gone. My medical record shows I had two seizures and went into a coma. At some later point I drifted back to consciousness.

I'm trying to talk to you! There is something in my mouth, going down my throat.

I plead with my eyes; I try to move my arms but they are tied down. I had been pulling IVs out so they had to use restraints. Looking from side to side I see Robert on my right, my mother on my left.

Please understand me—help me!

A team of physicians worked. One of them had called my mother who was listed as my next of kin at five Sunday morning. My mother called Robert. He brought what was left of my prescription drugs with him to the hospital.

They held a vigil at my bedside, waiting to see what would happen. Later, Robert said that I had so many IVs he wondered how they kept track of them.

A man was standing at the foot of my bed—one of the doctors. I heard him say, "I don't think she's going to make it."

A little later he said they had done all they could and that it was now up to me. I floated back into the unconscious.

Sunday passed and then, on Monday, I awoke. It was December 1993 and I was thirty-nine years old.[10]

10. Murphy, *Voices in Rain*, 153–55.

⟿

What kept me holding on? When in the hospital after taking the overdose, the battle was almost entirely unconscious because I was in a semi-to-completely-comatose state. It was fought down in a netherworld of mental, emotional, and spiritually unconscious forces. The doctor had said: "We've done all we can; it's now up to her. I don't think she's going to make it."

God only knows, literally, what went on in that realm of psychological battle. Did I fight for my life or try to convince God to just go ahead and let me die. I have no recollection.

PSYCHIATRY OUTPATIENT NOTE

December 30, 1993

Marcia just recently got out of the hospital after a serious suicide attempt, in fact she signed out AMA [against medical advice]. She had some complications as the result of the overdose of Imipramine. To begin with, she had two seizures and there were EKG changes that were worrisome. She had to have Coumadin because of a clotting problem. At any rate, she was monitored in the Cardiovascular Intensive Care Unit and transferred to a Medicine floor. To begin with she showed memory and thinking difficulties of an organic nature probably representative of anticholinergic delirium. This seemed to clear but as it did so she seemed emotionally labile and poorly controlled. She was irritable and impatient, and spoke of extreme distress related to being hospitalized and demanded to be released. Eventually she was so impatient with her physicians that she signed out but they were getting close to releasing her.

—Russell Noyes, MD

What led up to the suicide attempt? Did psychiatry fail me or was it my own fault or a combination of the two? Medical records from that time period reveal the biological orientation of my psychiatrists. At that time in my life the main focus was drugs for psychosis and drugs for depression. My doctors were highly skilled at administering these medications I must admit. The antipsychotic medications helped some in the early phase of my illness with partially stabilizing my emotions and blocking out some hallucinations. And then when Risperdal (risperidone) came out in 1994, that seemed to help more with intellectual clarity and reasoning. Nothing has ever cured my sleep disorder. I am often up at all hours of the night and take naps at any time of the day. And my episodic depressions seem to come and go on a regular basis regardless of which antidepressants are tried. My mood disorder has been continuous; early on, there was a periodic exploding upon the slightest provocation, along with the especially flat, dead, emotional emptiness in the center of my personality. They always said I had flat affect, which is a poker face without expression regardless of circumstances. Over the years I have been experiencing horrific physical pain and no one can tell, not the nurses, or physical therapists, or physicians. There isn't any facial expression in correspondence to my pain. Everyone thinks I'm fine.

It helps to look at my history leading up to the major suicidal event. The following medical record gives an example of my condition after I left a pseudo-religious cult when I was in my twenties where I experienced a psychotic break. In my thirties, I was given therapy sessions which focused on my problems but the sessions lacked psychological depth:

PROGRESS NOTE

February 13, 1986

Marcia made an appointment for today. She had written saying that she had quit her volunteer job, that she didn't think she was capable of working at this time, and planned instead to maintain her apartment and her personal hygiene, work on writing (which interests her) and work on having some social life. She finds that when she is around people she is extremely self-conscious and gets the feeling that people are putting thoughts in her mind and so on, so she becomes very uncomfortable, feels odd and awkward. But when she is apart from people she suffers a great deal of loneliness. At times, she has little motivation. She speaks of herself as rather constantly having some difficulty sleeping, headaches, and voices just outside her head that speak into her ears. Her affect may be slightly blunted. She asks a lot of questions, seeming to seek reassurance. She seems very sensitive. She jumps from one topic to another, doesn't seem to have much confidence in her opinions. She feels she is too disabled at this time to work, and I think this may be true. She says she has never really had very good rapport with any therapist. She has asked that appointments be on the basis of her feeling the need for them, so we are trying that for now.

—Russell Noyes, MD

Even though I had been through extensive trauma in earlier years there didn't seem to be methods for me to heal from these experiences. And my personal focus became what the culture promised to bring to me in happiness and fulfillment. I wanted to keep up my appearance, with weight control and exercise. I dreamed of a perfect romantic relationship that would culminate in a pleasant marriage. I struggled to find the right man and dated rather desperately, one after the other. It seemed futile because nothing worked out. I also went through paid employment positions and volunteer jobs one after the other. Being impulsive, I was very unstable, was impulsive, had little insight, and lacked understanding of spiritual wisdom. I had no desire to acquire wisdom or to even try to find it, it never crossed my mind. Instead, everything in my daily schedule skimmed over a material existence in the most shallow of manners as my mental condition deteriorated. The following is a medical record that further delineates how psychologically sick I was even though by outward appearances my doctors thought I looked rather good. I can't emphasize this point enough about outward appearance: though in a severely mentally disabled condition I was still able to keep up my grooming, weight control, nice hair, and wardrobe. But internally, psychologically, I was still incredibly sick and felt awful on a day-to-day basis.

The following medical record reveals an effort on my part to describe how I felt to my psychiatrist:

PROGRESS NOTE

August 8, 1986

Marcia made an appointment to come and see me today because over the past two months she has found herself exceedingly irritable and inpatient. She also reports that her mood is sometimes down and that she often hasn't much motivation. She feels the need to distance herself from people. There is a kind of negativity and bitterness. She finds herself reacting to people with resentment for no reason. Sometimes, she explodes over minor frustrations. She has wondered about a variety of circumstances that contribute to this, that there is something she has experienced [to cause it] which has fluctuated over time. She wonders: has she not very much support, has she been subject to criticism, has she been experiencing too much loneliness or too much isolation, would it be better if she were profitably occupied, could caffeine have anything to do with it? She is taking Navane 4mg a day and I'm suggesting doubling the dose and if this does not help in ten days to try Desipramine [an antidepressant]. Possibly taking three times a day with meals to reduce tendency to nausea that she has had with some antidepressants.

—Russel Noyes, MD

As you can see above, the answer provided for my distressing problems was to increase the medications. But in the defense of this psychiatrist, I will have to say that the field was not prepared to handle complex issues, at least in this Midwestern US region. Its insurance mandate's required that the patients be given drugs without in-depth analysis of the issues. At least, this is how it appears to me in retrospect. Afterall, it was the biological revolution in Psychiatry. The time of the broken brain model. It would have taken considerable time, maybe hours, months, of therapy, to explore what caused my irritability, impulsiveness, and depression. But time was not provided in the system. So, I was mostly left on my own to try to work out my difficulties by trial and error or by any answers I could muster through libraries. This was before the internet was in widespread use so I mainly sought information through libraries and bookstores. The following note further illustrates the medical response to my psychiatric problems:

PROGRESS NOTE

October 14, 1987

Marcia reported that her hallucinations have become worse and are very loud. She described herself as delusional, says that she gets the feeling that people think she's strange or that they hate her. The hallucinations she describes sounds like bell ringing. No voices but some muffled sounds possibly resembling them. She is not sleeping well and frequently awakens at 3:30 in the morning. She feels weak, doesn't like food much. She reports that her energy is low and her mood very low, and she was crying while talking to me. I suggested that she return to taking nortriptyline. To me this sounds like secondary depression which has returned. She may be a candidate for fluoxitane when that drug comes on the market. She came in because I had suggested seeing her once every six months and I'll see her again in another six months.

—Russell Noyes, MD

As noted above I was only invited to discuss my illness every six months at one point in my therapeutic relationship with this doctor. As a friend commented at one time: "You aren't getting any help." Maybe the kind of help I needed was beyond the scope of what this particular provider could offer at this point in his career.

Later on, things began to improve a bit as I describe in detail in my memoir, *Voices in the Rain: Meaning in Psychosis.*

My own preferences at this time in my life were to use antidepressants for depression, for example see this medical record:

PROGRESS NOTE

August 27, 1990

Marcia phoned to say that she is feeling depressed and wonders about taking an antidepressant. She said she has not been happy, that her energy is down, her interest is poor, she is not reading, doesn't like television, and sometimes doesn't want to be around her friends. She doesn't feel like doing very much and says she has used caffeine and sugar to try to make herself happy, but she doesn't like her situation and that has not worked very well. Her sleep is irregular as usual. Many nights she sleeps satisfactorily, other times she awakens in the night and can't get back to sleep. But when she uses Dalmane she feels groggy the next day, it has sort of a hangover effect. Once before she tried fluoxetine for about five days and felt it had strange effects. She would like to try it again and feels she did not give it a proper chance. I am suggesting that she try taking one every other day for five days and then doubling the dose. I have encouraged her to phone me about any side effects or questions about dose adjustment.

—Russell Noyes, MD

About two weeks later I phoned Dr. Noyes to tell him that I stopped taking the antidepressant because it didn't help and I would like, instead, to figure out what is causing me to be depressed and see if I could do something about it. Within twelve months I was then hospitalized for suicidal ideation all the while restarting antidepressants and was heavily medicated. Nothing seemed to help. I read Viktor E. Frankl's book *Man's Search for Meaning* at this time and remarked that it had had a great impact on me. Frankl was an Austrian psychiatrist, and founder of logotherapy; however, the lessons from his book was short lived. I soon forgot the message. My day-to-day struggles seemed overwhelming and nonending. I still cried often and continued to feel very down emotionally and felt the future was rather hopeless. It was hard for me to keep my morale up and my psychiatrist remarked that the antidepressants may be more of a source of encouragement than a real biological influence on my mood.

My social isolation before the suicidal event was about as bleak as anything could get. I had no family support. Any interaction between us caused me to feel intense distress, causing severe mental illness symptoms so I tried to distance myself from them. Female friend support was also almost completely nonexistent; I knew one woman but she was cold and aloof. There was one male, Robert, (a pseudonym, in my memoir *Voices in the Rain*) whom I spent time with: an occasional movie, eating out in restaurants, going to bars to listen to music. But in only a short time this one relationship turned sour. He was a Christian apostate who would put the Bible on the floor and literally stomp on it with his foot, cursing God and man. He had questionable character. I was left feeling desperate, abandoned, and could not figure out how to solve my problems. So, what was left? In my isolation was there anything remaining to sustain me?

My psychiatrist gave me the choice for how long the time would be between visits and at one point, I chose to stay away for an entire year. When I returned for an appointment, I told him as we walked down the hall in the clinic to his office: "I'm addicted to caffeine, nicotine, and sugar." Even though I had been living a lifestyle of altruism by working for social justice causes, my daily activities went without regular prayer to sustain me. I also lacked a vital connection to a religious community, and was unable to attend Sunday services. My physical addictions were idols. I relied on these three things to keep me going on a daily basis. Had I added daily prayer and scripture reading to psychiatric treatment I would not have been so bereft from the recovery process. These addictive chemical elements took the place of God and became my main focus which were only some temporary, quick-fix solutions. I definitely was going in the wrong direction which was an unhealthy one, heading toward what I would eventually find was an existential dead-end, the result of years of trying to live without God.

Eventually, I moved into a new neighborhood and I walked three blocks down the street to a mainline Protestant denomination church. Though initially ignored by most of its members, I did stick with it for nearly thirty years (as I pen this). Eventually, I made some friends, though very few in my own age bracket. Faith, then, became the predominant factor and motivation for living. And it was the institutional church—with all its flaws—which played a vital role in my reintegration within society as a whole. Without this, I barely survived psychologically and in a myriad of other ways. Back then, as I lay comatose in that hospital bed, the Lord must have convinced me to try again, to keep going, because God loved me and wished only the best for me. In addition, I had some work to do in the future.

For many years now I have struggled socially and at times lived only for my volunteer work and projects. I'm a writer, I've wanted to get things published; but not just anything. I have felt that I need to let people to know that belief in God has the potential to change our lives, give us purpose, and a reason to live. This is especially important for those who are afflicted with mental illness, my primary audience. That has been my field: psychiatry, psychology, and religion. The thought still, occasionally, crosses my mind, *things are not worth it; why endure?* Yes, suicide, still, occasionally, in some respects, looks rather attractive. For I still experience incredible suffering on not only the emotional level, but physically, too, with bodily ailments.

Viktor E. Frankl insisted that man searches for meaning and finds solace perhaps in a personal relationship with a significant other or in a career or both.[11] I would have to say that in addition, humans cannot exist without growing in relationship with God, and a divine meaning is found in knowing this God. After

11. Frankl, *Our Need for Meaning,* Noetic Films.

that, things will fall into place more naturally. We need our ducks in the right order. Man was made to be in relationship with his creator. God is our creator. And what does God require of us? I believe, to live each day to the fullest and to the best of our ability. Suicide, then, is an insult to God and we have no right to end our lives. Our position is one of subordination to our maker and those he has placed above us throughout our lives with which to guide us. A certain amount of insight and wisdom is required. Can we acknowledge the supremacy of a higher power and our dependence upon it? To help with our proper view of God we can try to imagine the vast power and greatness of the being that created the immense universe, i.e., the solar system, stars, and galaxies.

Over the years my publications have also touched upon the subject of societal rejection and how that has an impact on the emotional life of the mental patient which can cause suicidal behaviors. We need faith in God to help with this problem. Indeed, people treating others as though they are not worthy of respect can, in fact, kill them. Treating people as though they are subhuman destroys the victim's sense of worth to the point where they no longer wish to exist.

PSYCHIATRY OUTPATIENT NOTE

June 2, 1994

Marcia reports that 5 out of 7 days are pretty good; but 2 days are not good and on those days she finds she is irritable, her mood is low, she feels overwhelmed, finds it very difficult to function, and is bitter. She tells me that over the years she has done a bit of writing and has a rather substantial file of essays and stories that she has written, many from the perspective of someone who is mentally ill. She said she sent me something, and I have yet to receive it; but she may send others. This is something that she hadn't told me about, that is the file. I knew that she did writing and has aspired to do more. She was telling me that her IQ was tested in the Clinical Research

Center when participating in Dr. Nancy Andreasen's schizophrenia research study and that she has a full scale 127, with verbal and performance levels of 119 and 133. This shows that her intelligence is superior and would allow her to do graduate work. We talked some about the dose of risperidone and I suggested that some experimentation of the dose might be worthwhile. Trying the dose slightly higher as well as slightly lower might be a good thing to do. She will return in 3 months.

—Dr. Russell Noyes, MD

III

SUICIDE IN SCHIZOPHRENIA

PREVENTION | TREATMENTS

Artists may live for colors and designs. Authors, for words and books. If it's culinary, then baking and cooking, serving others and, of course, eating. So, we need to ask ourselves, what do I live for? Why do I get out of bed in the morning? What task is at hand.

We need to have compassion on ourselves. Each day is a new beginning. Sure, we make mistakes; but do we forgive ourselves or beat ourselves up? Do we forgive ourselves? God put us on this planet to learn, to grow into the kind of creature he wants to occupy his eternal kingdom. It takes years of struggle and lessons which are usually painful. Do we listen to the wise; do we seek out the wise to guide us?

But most important of all, perhaps not realizing that we need God is the problem. And, along with that, comes a reluctance to depend on the Christian community. It takes humility (something I am still working on) to acknowledge that we do not belong to ourselves; we who are Christians believe that we were bought at a price i.e., the cruel death by crucifixion of Christ, our savior, which then brought about new life through his resurrection from the dead. If we try to be independent from God, who is the source of life, this is a big and, can be, a fatal mistake. Therefore, what we conceive of as a god (which version) whom we choose to worship, matters, because our very lifestyles, our everyday choices as far as morals and values, and, indeed, our entire life trajectory, is the cumulative result of what we believe. We can go freely in unlimited directions, so it is important to know the right way. Our mental health depends on it.

The various religions proport to claim that their god is the one and only truth, as well as many people saying all religions are equally true, which is termed pluralism. How can we know which theology's god is the true God? I found through my personal experience that pluralism is false and that Jesus Christ has a unique role unequalled by any other person or thing. Phillip Cary, Professor of Philosophy, Eastern University, and Editor, Pro Ecclesia: A Journal of Catholic and Evangelical Theology says it succinctly:

> Pluralism is one of the most common ways for institutions and churches to go post-Christians these days. It is one thing to recognize the reality of different religions and respect people who are unlike you. It is another thing altogether to talk as if every religion is equally true. To take that second track is to abandon Christian faith, which has a very specific message to give to the world, centered on the uniqueness of Jesus Christ.
>
> The irony is that to give up on the uniqueness of your own religion is reduce the diversity in the world. Pluralism does not in fact honor difference but makes everybody look the same (they are all equally true, etc.). No real religion believes that. So, pluralism turns out to be a way of denying that different religions are unique and different. It is really a form of modern Western intellectual imperialism.[12]

My god is the God of Christianity and not pluralism. It is important to hear the Gospel preached each Sunday morning either on-line or in person at a church. When hearing something other than the Gospel preached, my brain gets defensive and has to then perform mental gymnastics to get itself in order. I need to be wired correctly so having a pastor who has the courage to preach the truth is very important.

Then there is forgiveness. Oh, my goodness, what an essential factor of recovery and healthy living. Carrying around grudges and hatred daily on our shoulders hampers one's lifestyle. Often, we suffer from memories of events involving various people that traumatize us. I have found that prayer is the only way to heal. I ask God to fill me with forgiveness to enable me to forgive the perpetrators who have afflicted me by physical and/or emotional abuse. And it takes time. Our memories will not evaporate, so coming to

12. Phillip Cary, email to author, 5/01/2023.

a place where we can forgive the person while still knowing what happened, can take years in the recovery process. We probably will never forget. But we can actively try to forgive and ask God to bless the person(s). I feel better knowing I've done all I can to try to forgive and I ask God to bless my enemies. When we ask God to bless the enemy, this unleashes powerful forces to mend relationships or in cases where reconciliation is not possible, at least protects us from further harm.

My dependence on the church is organic. As I struggled in my forties to find fellowship, attending worship services on Sunday mornings without socially connecting there, I almost killed myself. It happened one Sunday when I had returned home from a worship service at a neighborhood church. No one at the church that morning had spoken to me, no one reached out to me in love. No one there had cared about or acknowledged my presence within the church walls. I walked home dejected and alone in my misery. Upon reaching my apartment, suicidal thoughts flooded my consciousness. I felt to be in deep despair and hopelessness. I turned on my computer and opened the email program. Just then, out of the blue, I received an email from my psychiatrist, who is a Christian and attends a Lutheran church. I can't remember what he said; however, guided by the Spirit and unbeknownst to him, he saved me from further thoughts of suicide that morning by his email.

Yes, the Spirit moves in mysterious ways and we can't predict anything it does. Not having church people in my life was detrimental to my mental health. Not having Christians talk to me on a daily basis and care for me was devastating. I wanted to just end my life that Sunday. It took a long time to really connect socially, about 30 years of trial and error. And education. I did presentations for church Adult Education classes, wrote books and articles, gave talks for the congregation. *Please, don't be afraid of me. I am a human being like you.*

The people who attend churches all know someone with mental illness, be it a close relative or friend; however, the church has been reticent to actually deal with the issue. Mental illness and health has been hidden away in back rooms or closets, silently ignored, or openly denounced. Christians cling to organizations such as the National Alliance on Mental Illness (NAMI), an organization that will not acknowledge a spiritual component in mental illness. Christians, many of them, are reluctant to acknowledge that there is a spiritual world at all, with demonic entities battling against us humans and which play a part in mental distress. See my earlier writing for delineation of such concepts and descriptions. I maintain that the spiritual world is real and is a powerful factor in mental integrity or, conversely, its disintegration.

And medicine is important because the mind reacts chemically to stress organically in the physical brain. My psychosis has benefited from antipsychotic medication. The human is body, mind, and spirit, so we must treat the whole person which are all interrelated.

People will die, spiritually, without some connection to the church, be it an individual church member or some program, because the church is Christ's body, however imperfect. We starve without this connection. Prayer helps. Talking to someone helps. Finding a companion or friend. Sunday worship is not always accessible because maybe a person doesn't own a vehicle. Or it's too far to walk on foot. Or there might be physical health problems. Sometimes, people need assistance. If the church people are so wrapped up in their own lives and don't want to give a helping hand, this is deplorable. It is not what Christ meant for his community.

The church I attend gives out food, some members have given me clothing. I eventually got rides to church; but it took many, long years to reach this point. Some people who've committed suicide never made this connection through no fault of their own. Sometimes, the church has failed to offer a welcome to those walking in their doors. The church I attend now is very enthusiastic about welcoming newcomers each Sunday morning, but for the shy newcomer this can be a bit overwhelming at times. We also need gentle, sensitive methods for reaching out to help the newcomer feel valued. Not everyone is an extrovert.

There are several things that give hope to the hopeless. One is by reading the scriptures every morning before starting one's day's activities. I read my Bible as I drink my morning coffee. Our hope comes from belief in God and the scriptures give encouragement. Before my major suicide attempt, I did not have this habit. My daily life was raw and unprotected. However, with scripture reading and, in addition, morning prayer, I ask God for help and protection for the day, and also for guidance. After the attempt, I began to ask for grace, faith, and hope on a daily basis. God provides.

My first step forward in my writing that, in addition, began my recovery process, was when I sat down at an electric typewriter one day in my livingroom and typed out the Lord's Prayer. For the readers who are not religious and who are unfamiliar with this prayer, I will put the full text here:

> Our Father, who art in Heaven, hallowed be thy name. Thy kingdom come; thy will be done, on earth as it is in Heaven. Give us this day our daily bread and forgive us our debts as we forgive our debtors. And lead us not into temptation; but deliver us from evil. For thine is the kingdom and the power and the glory forever and ever. In Jesus Christ's name I pray, Amen.

Additionally, along with having good daily habits, healthy relationships are vitally important. For me, this was not always the case. Before the major suicide attempt, I was in a relationship with a cruel man who would terrorize my cat by trying to stomp on it; and who would emotionally and physically abuse me. He used profanity often and cursed God, and physically abused the Bible. He eventually confessed that he only dated me because he wanted to see my sister, they had been in the same high school class. He wanted to go to my family gatherings to see her. He was using me. He didn't care about me at all. The emotional abuse came to a head when he said he was breaking up with me because I could not stand the sub-zero cold temperatures one winter night when he wanted to spend time in a warehouse with his band member friends and I demanded to be taken home. I felt completely abandoned by someone I had put my misguided trust in. That left me with no social support whatsoever. There became a deep, dark void.

Now in my life I have a friend who is loving and kind and who sacrifices himself for my wellbeing. He is considerate and cares about my needs and I care about his. This person believes in God and prays, reads his Bible, and we attend church together. He has self-discipline and is a good example. He told me that he will protect me and not let anyone hurt me. He is kind to animals, a neighborhood cat loves him and it trusted him on sight, rubbing against him. Having this friend has made all he difference in the world. Because of this friendship I have strength to continue my battle against physical pain in my lower limbs which is often excruciating. I want to keep living to support this friend because he depends on me, we have a mutual dependence. I have learned to endure great suffering because people need me. I will stay alive and not commit suicide because I need to assist others.

But mostly, I want to stay alive to love God. I want to love and serve God through Jesus Christ, his son. Being connected to Christ will allow me to produce fruit for the heavenly kingdom. Serving God will be in obedience to God's commandments: *You shall love the Lord your God with all your heart, and with all your soul, and with all your strength, and with all your mind; and your neighbor as yourself.* (Luke 10:27 RSV)

My work has given me a great reason to live; however, without the social aspect of feeling connected to a loving person or religious group I can't do the work. My ministry to advocate for those with mental illness led me to make new friends in and outside the institutional church. For example, I've made many friends in the downtown area of Iowa City by serving God, some of whom are homeless. And, as an aside, the homeless are incredibly strong-minded survivors, using their wits to get by day to day on very little or no resources in the face of societal rejection. This topic, however, will be addressed in a future writing project.

The field of psychiatry has, historically, had its problems. Currently, however, strides have been made. Many patients believe that the modern-day medications prevent them from hearing voices, voices that terrorize them otherwise. When a psychiatrist uses part of the sessions for psychotherapy in addition to the med check, this is ideal, which I've personally experienced. Email communication is also very helpful for the patient to report progress and/or problems. I know all this takes time which is in short supply when doctors are pressured to see as many patients as humanly possible within a limited time span.

And what kind of psychotherapy? All depends on the therapist's worldview or perspective. When the therapist is atheist or is a non-theologically oriented person, his methods will reflect this sometimes leading to a certain type of advice. A therapist cannot impose their own religious beliefs either, but they can still help the patient discover the best path to take.

What do doctors need to ask the patients? I believe a doctor could ask: when do you feel the most energy in your living, an energy that makes you feel especially alive? What activity? And, where do you meet new friends? What organizations or places can you go to to be around those who share the same interests? Also, how can you find an interesting project to focus on which will make you feel worthwhile? How can you maintain your physical health as well as, your psychological health? Dear patient, do you care enough to make some effort on your own behalf?

Something that needs to be clearly understood by the psychiatric community is that financial insecurity, including homelessness, will have a big impact on their patients' mental health and contributes to a lack of well-being. Just ask yourself: how well do you function on an empty stomach? Survival, i.e., finding food, clothing, and shelter can be more important to a patient than the philosophical musings of an erudite psychotherapist.

The medically assisted suicide movement is an unfortunate development and is not God's intention for mankind. God gave us precious life. We humans are not to end it ourselves. It is true that suffering is difficult; but there are things we can do to help us cope: pray, listen to music, take baths, socialize with those we love, for example. There are lots of ways to cope with pain, be it physical or not. A religious notion is that suffering purifies us in some way, so it is not in vain. It also brings us closer God since Jesus knew what suffering was more than anyone, on the cross. I speak as one who suffers with a physical ailment, my lower limbs are almost always in pain and I have fantasized about ending my life many times. But I have found that listening to Christian music on YouTube really makes a big difference in my outlook. Going to church as much as possible also helps, and socializing with good, strong people who stand up for justice and mercy. When someone from a religious community reaches out and connects with me, showing God's love and concern, this is of great importance. We cannot walk this road alone.

The assisted suicide movement's reasoning is all about control: you, yourself, are in control. Not God. *You* decide how much suffering is enough. *You* decide when to end life on *your own terms*. However, the Bible teaches in the Ten Commandments: *You shall not kill.* (Exodus 20:13 RSV) This is applicable to do not murder which includes *yourself.* People using assisted suicide believe that death will make them happy. *Wrong idea.* Assisted suicide is all about *me, me, me!* What *I* want! This is all very self-centered. There is nothing here about God, who, alone, decides our time of death.

Overall, we cannot avoid suffering, it is here every day if not physically, then emotionally. We can try to ignore it by dulling the feelings with alcohol and/or drugs. There are many ways we try to escape. For those without religious faith nothing makes sense. However, I believe that there is a God and this God put suffering in our lives for a reason. Let God do his work, to transform, making us new. For someday we will be heavenly creatures, reflecting Christ's image, all for the glory of God.

Bibliography

Center for Disease Control. "Disparities in Suicide." https://www.cdc.gov/
suicide/facts/disparities-in-suicide.html#:~:text=Men%20aged%20
75%20and%20older,compared%20to%20other%20age%20groups.
———. "Suicide Ideation is Higher Among People with Disabilities."
https://www.cdc.gov/suicide/facts/disparities-in-suicide.
html#:~:text=Limited%20data%20are%20available%20on,in%20the%20
general%20U.S.%20population).
Frankl, Viktor. YouTube Noetic Films. *Our Need for Meaning and Purpose.*
https://youtu.be/lDo9bOoHtoo.
Hor, Kahyee and Mark Taylor. "Suicide and Schizophrenia: A Systematic Review
of Rates and Risk Factors." Journal of Psychopharmacology 24 (4) (2010)
81–90. https://www.ncbi.nlm.nih.gov/pmc/articles/PMC2951591/.
Murphy, Marcia A. *The Collected Writings of Marcia A. Murphy: Christus
Magnus Medicus Sanat.* Eugene: Resource Publications, 2020.
Palmer, Brian A. et al. "The Lifetime Risk of Suicide in Schizophrenia: A
Reexamination." Archives of General Psychiatry, 62 (3) (2005) 247–53.
Patural, Amy. Brain & Life. "How Treatment for Chronic Pain Can Help Reduce
Suicide Risk." https://www.brainandlife.org/articles/living-with-pain.
Shapiro, Mark. "Suicide Rates Spike in Spring, Not Winter."
https://www.hopkinsmedicine.org/news/articles/suicide-rates-spike-in
-spring-not-winter.

www.ingramcontent.com/pod-product-compliance
Lightning Source LLC
Chambersburg PA
CBHW070734030726
47601CB00001B/22